> "Surely goodness and mercy shall follow me all the days of my life; and I will dwell in the house of the Lord forever."
> **-Psalm 23:6**

Real Life Testimonies

21-Day Inspirational Devotional

REAL LIFE TESTIMONIES

Copyright @2022 Brenda Burton

Real Life Testimonies
21-Day Inspirational Devotional

All rights reserved. This book or any portion thereof may not be reproduced or used in any manner whatsoever without the express written permission of the publisher except for the use of brief quotations in a book review.

Published in The United States Of America

Book Development & Editing
Purpose Writers LLC
Berneka@PurposeWriters.Org
www.PurposeWriters.Org

Author's Contact Information
brendaburton349@yahoo.com

Scriptures are taken from the VERSION®, NIV® Copyright® 1973, 1978, 1984, 2011 by Biblical, Inc.® Used by permission. All rights reserved worldwide. The ESV® Bible, The Holy Bible, English Standard Version®. ESV® Text Edition: 2016. Copyright® 2001 by Crossway, a publishing ministry of Good News Publishers. The ESV® text has been reproduced in cooperation with and by permission of Good News Publishers.

Quotes: Good Reads & Google

For related resources and information on booking the author to speak, please submit request to email.

"Never give up hope. All things are working for your good. One day, you'll look back on everything you've been through and thank God for it."

— **Germany Kent**

REAL LIFE TESTIMONIES

Author's Autograph

_____

TABLE OF CONTENTS

REAL LIFE TESTIMONIES

Dedication	10
Introduction	12
Day 1: Unfaithfulness	15
Day 2: Selling Illegal Drugs	18
Day 3: Verbal Abuse	22
Day 4: Insecurity	25
Day 5: Physical Abuse	28
Day 6: Same Sex Attraction	32
Day 7: Molestation	35
Day 8: Jealousy	38
Day 9: Love	40
Day 10: Self-Confidence	42
Day 11: Saying No	46
Day 12: Failure	49
Day 13: Rejection	52
Day 14: Stuck In The Past	55
Day 15: Suicide	57
Day 16: Theft	61
Day 17: Trauma	64
Day 18: Unforgiveness	67
Day 19: Overthinking	69
Day 20: Negativity	71
Day 21: Health	73

> "The Lord is good to all, and His tender mercies are over all His works."
> **~Psalm 145:9**

REAL LIFE TESTIMONIES

This Book Belongs To:

_____

DEDICATION

REAL LIFE TESTIMONIES

I dedicate this book to God, my husband, children, close family, and friends. I am blessed to have you in my life. Thank you, God, for giving me the strength to make every test manifest into a testimony. Thank you for endowing me with supernatural strength and courage to write this book because I can do nothing without you.

To my loving husband, thank you for just being there by my side through it all. I love and appreciate how much you push and support me in everything I do. My life feels so complete with you, and I am happy to have you.

To my children, you are my #1 support, and I'm so blessed to be your mother. Thank you for enduring every season of my life with me and never holding my mistakes or shortcomings against me. You make my heart smile, and I couldn't imagine life without you.

To my friends and family, you are all appreciated more than you will ever know. Thank you for never giving up on me and believing in me when I didn't believe in myself. I appreciate every call, text, and phone conversation you have utilized to encourage me.

I love and thank you all for being on this journey with me.

INTRODUCTION

REAL LIFE TESTIMONIES

There is so much power in a testimony. No matter what you have been through, there is nothing like telling someone how you got out. Believe it or not, your testimony has the power to change someone's entire life. It has the potential to set someone free from the bondage that has held them captive for years.

The moment you choose to open your mouth and share what the Lord has done in your life is the same moment that you invite someone to draw closer to God or help their faith increase. Everyone needs reassurance now and then to remind them to hold on to God's unchanging hand. Whether you are battling cancer, going through a toxic divorce, missing a deceased loved one, or experiencing a tough season, one testimony can give you supernatural strength and clarity about what God is doing in your life. My life has not always been full of sunshine and rainbows.

I have suffered much, endured a lot, and survived many things that could've killed me, but I have been inspired to share my testimonies about how God stepped in right on time for me. This book allows readers to hear what I have overcome in my life. Each testimony is transparent, authentic, and speaks my truth. Readers will receive encouragement, comfort, peace, and spiritual empowerment to continue trusting God with their life.

This devotional connects readers back to God through hearing how God released favor, grace, healing, and breakthrough in my life.

"The Lord is good, a stronghold in the day of trouble; and He knows those who trust in Him."
~Nahum 1:7

REAL LIFE TESTIMONIES

Day 1: Unfaithfulness

Unfortunately, I don't have the innocent little princess story that women have because I was not innocent at all. As a matter of fact, I was the complete opposite. From a very young age, early teens, I was very unfaithful due to the brokenness and betrayal I experienced so young. My hurt always led me to do whatever was done to me, and this is how I initially became a habitual cheater and liar in my relationships. I had no compassion for anyone who crossed or betrayed me in a friendship or relationship, mutual or intimately. If you crossed me, you were definitely going to be crossed in a major way that would rip your heart out. I was not ashamed to be considered a whore because I did whatever I wanted, and it was no secret. The feeling of being cheated on or betrayed in any form made me feel worthless and unwanted, so the way I paid each person back was to lay up with whoever whenever and gain some kind of feeling of "I got them back." This was not the lifestyle that any young lady should have lived, but when you are torn, damaged, and hurt, you don't have any standards in your life. You don't realize that the best get back is to heal, mature, and go after your purpose and destiny as you disconnect from those who do not see your value. I didn't love myself, and it affected me terribly that I depended on others to love me. This pain, rejection, and hurt caused me great distress.
I was causing harm to my body and could have died playing with my life physically, sexually, mentally,

REAL LIFE TESTIMONIES

and emotionally. However, God turned my life around, and I am grateful for his grace and mercy. I was delivered after growing closer to a family member that was much older and wiser than me. She was saved and had a passion about her personal relationship with God. The closer we became, the more I was inspired to get to know God. I looked up to her very much and started to attend church services with her. During every service, I was so anxious to repent for my actions. I became godly sorrowful and desired more change in my life, so I decided to be baptized and give my life to Christ. Change did not happen overnight, and I was still a mess in areas of my life. However, I wanted to change for real, so I continued to come to church and pursue God with everything in me. I knew over time that he would clean me up and make me new. I remember my flesh still wanting to do things that I was begging God to free me from, and he would reveal the spirit of lust that was still lurking over my life. As I pursued him, he started to deliver me, and the things I thought I couldn't stop doing began to fall off me. When God steps in, he makes all things new, your mind, body, and soul. No one else may not have forgiven me and loved me despite my past, but he did. Whatever you do, do not remain stuck living an unfaithful wildlife. You are only hurting yourself, and this can only lead to destruction. Give God your life! Come to him just as you are, dirty and unworthy, and allow him to make you over again. He did it for me, and he can do it for you.

REAL LIFE TESTIMONIES

Study Scripture: Proverbs 3:3-5

REAL LIFE TESTIMONIES

Day 2: Selling Illegal Drugs

I started selling drugs as a teenager when I was about 14 years old. My first boyfriend, who was about three years older than me, was my everything back then, and whatever he asked me to do, I was down. We ran the streets together, sold drugs to make extra money, and eventually, trafficking became a part of our lives as well to make money. Although we did this a lot, we never got caught, and this was clearly a sign that God has his hand on my life. We hung in our relationship for years until it became abusive. It finally ended after him brutally stabbing me one night, and he ended up in jail. I was devasted by the abuse I had to suffer at his hands because I loved him, but I was also devasted because I had to learn how to navigate life with him, completely erased from it. I was still a hustler because of the years I had done it with him, but it was time to get back to the money. However, I was not alone; I started a new relationship with a man who was also in the streets at the time, which is my husband today. Our relationship didn't begin right because we were both unstable, living in separate places and trying to make a living individually and separately. Over time, we moved in together to build our family together, but as soon as I thought things were coming together, he got into some trouble and was on house arrest. This situation left him jobless and unable to contribute to our family's financial needs. We had a new baby, my second child, and we were forced to live off my one income,

REAL LIFE TESTIMONIES

which was only enough to cover the rent. I had to do something to make things work, at least until he was able to go back to work. We both decided to go back to selling drugs, and we did it day and night. He couldn't leave the house much, but that was fine; we sold drugs anyway we saw fit right from home. This lasted for a couple of years until he was allowed to find a pretty decent job around his placement. I ended up finding Jesus, and prayer became very dear to me. I didn't want anything else to do with selling drugs and made that clear to him, especially after our 8-year-old daughter started having dreams about the system coming to take our children out of our custody. I told him that he was not allowed to bring drugs back into our home if he was going to continue selling them. He didn't give it up right away, but he respected our children and home. Somehow, God allowed me and my husband to come into a lump sum of money, and he gave up selling drugs for good. My daughter stopped having those dreams, and my husband and I have seen the hand of God on our lives financially non-stop. All money is not good money, and although we feel like we have to do what we have to do to survive, there is always a better route. God is a provider, but he needs you to trust in him at all times, even in the struggle, to come through for you. We didn't get caught because of the grace and mercy over our lives, but you may run out of grace and end up dead or sentenced to prison time. This is not the will of God for your life, so get out now while you can.

REAL LIFE TESTIMONIES

Work on creating a strategy to go back to school, start a new job, or launch a business that will work for you financially. Selling drugs or transporting them does not promise you a future, yet it promises you an opportunity to cancel all your dreams, goals, and the purpose that God has over your life.

REAL LIFE TESTIMONIES

Study Scripture: Matthew 6:33

REAL LIFE TESTIMONIES

<u>Day 3: Verbal Abuse</u>

Words have always affected me for some reason, good or bad. I always felt esteemed and loved when people said things that encouraged, inspired, or encouraged me. However, it was always hard for me to get back up whenever words were used to tear me down. I would literally break down emotionally and mentally when I was spoken to like a dog on the streets. I was verbally abused for years, and it was by someone I loved. It is hard to be spoken evil of or to by others, but verbal abuse hits different when it is done by someone you have committed to love and stand by in your life. When it was other people speaking to or against me negatively to hurt my feeling and break me down, I didn't like it, and it still hurt me, but I was able to brush it off and move on much easier. However, the man I loved always found a way to make me feel like I was a piece of dirt or nothing at all. Although I would get back at him with my slick words to defend myself, I was always the one left crying and depressed for days after hearing him tear me down with his words. Sadly, he would get up the next day as if nothing had ever happened. He would pretend he had never said anything destructive and nasty to me and go about his day as usual. That hurt me to the core because I at least deserved a sincere apology and his willingness to change. He could not see how deep his verbal abuse cut me. His words made me feel ugly, insecure, stupid, unworthy, and unwanted. I felt so alone even when he was lying right next to

REAL LIFE TESTIMONIES

me because his verbal abuse caused me to feel unsafe and unprotected. I also realized that his lack of love and compassion towards me caused me to dislike myself. I didn't love myself because I was so broken down from the battle between me and his words that repeated over and over in my head until, eventually, I believed everything he said about me. He was fighting his own demons and unwilling to work on himself, so it was easy to beat me down with negative words than it was for him to become a better man. I had no idea how to help him or myself, but God always finds a way to bring peace during our storms. One day, while I was preparing a meal for us, he started to fight with me verbally. Everything in me wanted to repeat this toxic cycle of arguing back with him and adding fuel to the fire, but God stepped in this time. I heard a small voice tell me to be quiet. I decided to be obedient and allow God to fight for me. In my time of quietness, God revealed to me that it takes two to argue. The more I remained quiet, the quicker the argument ended. I started to apply this powerful principle to my life, which impacted me. I heard God's voice over all the negative words thrown at me. The more I heard God, the more I slipped into peace. There is no need to fight anyone back because it's a setup to fail and hinder your process of getting to purpose. The tools I have used to help me conquer verbal abuse are prayer, silence, and self-control. I have overcome the negativity that tried to break me down. I thank God for healing me and teaching me how to maintain my peace.

REAL LIFE TESTIMONIES

Study Scripture: Luke 6:45

REAL LIFE TESTIMONIES

Day 4: Insecurity

I can really tell you when it started, but insecurity has always played a role in my life since I was a little girl. It was extremely easy for me to feel ugly, unworthy, or as if I was good enough for something for someone when someone said or did something to me that hurt my feelings. My insecurity stayed at an all-time high, even though many people had no idea I battled with this. It got even worse after my physical abuse incident happened. I lost more of my confidence, self-worth, and self-esteem. The scars left on my body made me feel very unattractive and as if I would never be worth a man being faithful. People would stare at me, and this made me feel more insecure. A statement was made to me that I was too insecure and was lucky even to have the man I had in my life by a family member. This broke me down to the core mentally and emotionally; however, it made me better. It was very hurtful, but I decided to give this pain to Jesus, and he began to direct me to my healing. I realized that I was insecure, and I needed to love myself. I had to acknowledge the truth about what I was really dealing with and take responsibility for thinking low about myself. I had to learn how to forgive those who called out this spirit I was dealing with because God used them to show me my truth. Although it hurt, it also helped when I allowed it to. I learned what confidence really meant, and my life has never been the same. I will never forget a woman of God who said to me, "baby, Jesus has scars too!"

REAL LIFE TESTIMONIES

This statement changed my whole perspective, and I thank God for the love and value I have for myself today. Stop devaluing yourself and defeat the spirit of insecurity over your life. You are not beneath; you are above. You are not unworthy; you are worth more than gold. You are not ugly; your beauty is far beyond looks, weight, and the size you wear. God loved everything about you, and you should embrace this wholeheartedly. Insecurity is a fruit of Satan's, and he desires to use it to destroy you mentally, emotionally, and physically. Don't give him that power or authority! Fight back with faith to build your self-worth and dignity back up. Stand strong on how amazing you are and how precious you are to God.

REAL LIFE TESTIMONIES

Study Scripture: Proverbs 3:15-18

REAL LIFE TESTIMONIES

Day 5: Physical Abuse

Physical abuse started in my life at the age of 14. I dated a young man who was three years older than me, so he was more experienced and mature than I was when it came to dating. He spoiled me, but I was also mistreated and physically abused by him. My mother didn't really know the age difference between us, at least not the truth, so our relationship started wrong anyway. However, I stayed with him for six long years and endured what no teenage girl should. We went through pure hell during those six years, one child together, one stillborn baby, too many fights to count, but the last one almost cost me my life. I was stabbed multiple times, which left lifetime scars on my body, I was considered disabled, and I was told that I would never be able to use my hands to take care of myself or my daughter. He also stabbed my daughter and could have taken her life in this mist of this tragic outburst. This physical abuse damaged me in more ways than I can express, but mentally and emotionally, I was torn and distressed. However, God still got the glory out of this. Not only did we survive this abuse, but I was able to use my hands, and he was arrested for his actions toward us. I cannot do everything I desire with my hands, but God has healed me through this journey and has given me the ability to utilize my hands in ways I couldn't. I hate this happened to me, but I do not hate him. I learned how to forgive and move on with my life. I am here to tell my story, and so are you.

REAL LIFE TESTIMONIES

Do not hold unforgiveness towards those who violated you physically and hurt you. It took God to help me forgive this man, so turn to him to help you too.

REAL LIFE TESTIMONIES

Study Scripture: 1 Corinthians 13:4-7

"Every good gift and every perfect gift is from above, and comes down from the Father of lights, with whom there is no variation or shadow of turning."
~James 1:17

REAL LIFE TESTIMONIES

Day 6: Same Sex Attraction

I have never been with another woman sexually, but I have wanted to be with one and felt like being with one was better than being with a man. I was unsure about where this strange desire came from because I always wanted to be with a man, and I knew it was wrong for same-sex relationships in the eyes of God. I was reminded of how this spirit slipped into my life while writing. When I was about nine years old, my mother would allow us to stay at different family members' houses. A male family member molested me, but then a female family member molested me. We didn't visit this particular family member's house too much, so the incident didn't happen more than once, but I remember clearly how uncomfortable she made me feel. However, I didn't know it was wrong for another woman to violate the body of another female because I was too young to recognize the severity of what was happening to me. This moment caused me to be unsure about who I was supposed to be attracted to. It affected my sexual appetite and caused me frustration internally that I never really spoke about to others. I was battling a generational curse that I needed to defeat before it defeated me. This spirit tormented me up until I was tired of dealing with it. I prayed about it repeatedly, but I still felt it creeping up on me when I least expected it to. I had no clue how to break free from this, but Hod always shows up right on time. I was connected to a pastor through a mutual friend who was willing

REAL LIFE TESTIMONIES

to facilitate a deliverance service to help me break free, and I decided to attend. This night changed my life forever. I was told to confess my battle and to call out the names of every person who had sexually violated me. I was instructed to forgive them and let it go that night. I literally almost threw up my insides going through this deliverance process, but I was so glad to get up and walk out free. Please do not carry your abusers around with you from day to day, believing you are hurting them because you are not. In order to defeat the demonic spirits that have attached themselves to you through the sexual violations, you must confess, forgive, and allow God to heal and deliver you.

REAL LIFE TESTIMONIES

Study Scripture: Leviticus 18:22

_____

_____

_____

_____

_____

_____

_____

_____

_____

_____

_____

_____

_____

_____

_____

REAL LIFE TESTIMONIES

Day 7: Molestation

After my mother left a terrible relationship with my father, she met another man that caught her attention. She fell in love with this guy and started a new family with him, including me. She had another baby with him, which is my brother, four years later. However, this relationship didn't last either. By the time my brother was two years old, they had split up. My mother went her separate way, but she still allowed us to visit him on the weekends. I was around this man for years, so I considered him my daddy. However, my weekends transitioned from fun to pain. I was eight years old when the molestation started. I would receive notes saying, "can I rape you tonight?" I was being touched inappropriately in my vaginal area and having a grown man's penis rubbed against my vagina. I would cry because I was scared and because the things he started to do hurt bad. This went on for some time until my mother started letting us go to another family member's house when she had to go out etc. I never told my mother what he did to me until I was thirteen years old. I was completely hurt, embarrassed, and too humiliated to tell her. I didn't know if I had done something to make him do this to me, and I loved him as a father. I couldn't believe that he would ever do something harmful to me like this. Sadly, every time he saw me, he pretended like he loved and missed me and never did anything wrong to me. My mother didn't blame me for his actions; instead, she comforted me. She assured me that she would've stepped in to protect me if she knew he was doing this to me. I never hated him for it, but I always wanted to ask why. He passed away, so I never got my answer, but I forgave him anyway. God helped me understand what I couldn't, and he kept my heart pure towards him. God was with me the entire time I cried and hurt over this, and he is with you as well. He will never leave us in distress and brokenness over something we had no control over, so turn to him for strength, forgiveness, and healing.

REAL LIFE TESTIMONIES

Study Scripture: 1 Corinthians 6:9

_____

_____

_____

_____

_____

_____

_____

_____

_____

_____

_____

_____

_____

_____

_____

_____

REAL LIFE TESTIMONIES

Day 8: Jealousy

I not only battled with insecurity, but I also battled with the spirit of jealousy. Most of my jealous tendencies were in young adult life after going through so much hell, being cheating on, and being scarred physically from a domestic violence relationship. This made me clingy and always read to show out on someone who acted like they wanted what I had. I was very insecure, and this made my jealousy level even worse. I wanted to know my man's every move, would track him down., search his phone, and was ready to pop up and fight wherever I needed to if I felt like he was cheating or lying to me about his location. It took me a while to heal and be delivered from this type of behavior, and although God is still working on me, I am free from much of the toxic behaviors I shared in the previous sentence. This is not cute for any male or female, and you are not in control of what someone will or will not do to you in a relationship. Jealousy does not keep a man or a woman; it actually causes them to run away eventually. Jealousy can lead to tragedy or even death, so go to God in prayer and ask for deliverance. I was honest with God about what I needed help with and was sincere about my request. Jealousy is also wickedness, so be free from it before t destroys your life.

REAL LIFE TESTIMONIES

Study Scripture: Proverbs 27:4

REAL LIFE TESTIMONIES

Day 9: Love

I love hard period! When I say I love you, I really mean it, but there was a time in my life when I didn't love myself, and even if I thought I loved others, I really wasn't because I hated myself and the things I had gone through in my life. I hated the way I looked, the scars left on my body, and I hated what people thought about me because of who I was and how I looked to them. Love was absent from my life, and I didn't understand how powerful it was until I found out that it was the greatest commandment. Before I could love anyone, even myself, I needed to fall in love with God and embrace what he felt, said, and believed about me. He was always supposed to be my first love anyway, but I was too busy trying to give others his position. As I began to walk with God, I realized how much "love" meant to him, that I needed to forgive myself and move forward in the spirit of love genuinely towards everyone, even my enemies. I couldn't love anybody right without starting with myself first! Now, I can honestly say that I know my worth. I know who I am, and I love everything about me, the good, bad, ugly, and everything else that comes with me! Learn to love yourself first and work on your love for others. It is necessary for your purpose, assignments, and future. Love conquers all.

REAL LIFE TESTIMONIES

Study Scripture: Proverbs 10:12

REAL LIFE TESTIMONIES

Day 10: Self-Confidence

When things started happening to me at an early age, my self-confidence was broken in many ways. I believed whatever a man or an enemy said about me because you hear everyone's lies over God's truth when you lack self-confidence. Besides battling with how I looked, I was unsure about anything being positive or beautiful about me. I never considered the beauty in my personality, my heart towards people, and how caring I was. I was too focused on my scars that I missed seeing how amazing I was despite the scars and everything I had gone through. But God is indeed the healer to all things, and he works everything together for your good. In 2016, he came to me in a dream and said, "you shall have confidence, and when you speak, mountains will move!" I was encouraged, and I knew he was building me up to where I was weak. God will give you things in parables because he can't give you everything at one time. I had to learn that we don't always know right what he says or means right away, but he always reveals it in time. Today, he has given me so much confidence. I believe in myself, his truth, his unfailing word, and I trust that everything he said he would do, he will do it. I'm a living testimony because I had no clue where I would be today without him & his promises for my life! I reflect on the good things in my life & what God has done, and it gives me so much peace, joy, faith, & confidence that only he can provide. Once you have faith enough to speak to your

REAL LIFE TESTIMONIES

mountains, it shall move! Faith is the key to moving your mountain. When you really start speaking, mountains begin to move, and everything that has blocked you from believing in yourself is destroyed.

REAL LIFE TESTIMONIES

"Good and upright is the Lord."
~Psalm 25:8

REAL LIFE TESTIMONIES

Study Scripture: Hebrews 10:35

REAL LIFE TESTIMONIES

Day 11: Saying No

I really never knew how to say no to people, even when I needed to. My heart is big, but so was my insecurity, so being the yes lady made me feel like I would keep friends, people would love me more, and I would be accepted because of what I gave them. I would go out of my way for others and do things, even if I didn't do anything for myself. I put myself last in many situations because my heart was big, and my priorities were completely out of order. If someone asked, I did it no matter what the circumstances were. I did this for a long time, not realizing that people never put me first the way I did for them. When I recognized this was a form of abuse and self-inflicted wounds, I felt bad. I became angry when people I put first were always putting me last. I couldn't tell anyone no until God started to open my eyes to see what I was doing to myself and allowing others to do to me as well. When God is continuously working on you, you will eventually see that it's affecting you, leaving you heartbroken, torn, feeling used, etc., because you have given, poured, and did your all for others, but you are still left without. I was told in 2018 that God said to stop doing things for people so they could love you. I was told that God truly loves me unconditionally, and I immediately found peace and learned how to start saying no. I don't feel bad anymore when I say it; however, I feel peace, positive energy, & power, and no fear. I consider myself, family, and my priorities before giving anything. I also acknowledge God first

REAL LIFE TESTIMONIES

before saying yes to a request, and I encourage you to do the same. Break free from the bondage of saying yes all the time without thinking, evaluating, and considering what you have to do for yourself first. Avoid becoming selfish and nasty towards people but say yes when God releases you too. Don't apologize for setting boundaries in your life, and always remember that saying yes to everyone does not make you special or worth anything to them. Learn to embrace self-discipline, courage, and principles that will keep you from being stressed and heartbroken.

REAL LIFE TESTIMONIES

Study Scripture: 2 Timothy 1:7

REAL LIFE TESTIMONIES

Day 12: Failure

The spirit of failure played a huge role in my life for years. It seemed as if no matter what I tried at one point in my life, I failed. It is heartbreaking and discouraging to pursue, build, or put your time into something that crumbles or the door slams in your face. Every time I turned around, I was failing at something I worked hard to see manifest in my life, and it caused me to slip into depression and fear. I started to become afraid of even trying anything or being too excited about anything I wanted to accomplish. I began to feel like I was not good enough or deserving of anything good in my life, and that was the enemy trying to distract me from keeping my faith and defeating failure. I am so thankful that I turn to God in prayer, asking him to help me see where I am going wrong and strengthen me in this area. I started reading and believing what God promised me in his words and has promised you too. He said he would give us the desires of our hearts. He made it clear that when we diligently seek after and love him, there are no good things that he will keep from us. Failure continued to defeat me because I needed to reposition the way I perceived things, make sure I was submitted to God and his will for my life, and walk-in faith no matter where things didn't go the way I planned. Never allow yourself to sink into discouragement because things are not going right. Sometimes, those things are not what God wants for you. Do not quit pursuing what you believe God has called you to do

REAL LIFE TESTIMONIES

or manifest in your life. Wake up every day, put God first, acknowledge him in all your ways, and go after your dreams. Anything is possible with God and when you believe.

REAL LIFE TESTIMONIES

Study Scripture: 2 Corinthians 12:9-10

REAL LIFE TESTIMONIES

__Day 13: Rejection__

The spirit of rejection also tried to claim my life. There were many days I felt like nobody loved me or wanted me around, even my own mother. I treated her badly many times innocently because of my own thoughts and feelings of being rejected, and I was wrong. The times she did do things that made me feel unwanted, I still owed her love and respect. I was unhappy about how I looked because I looked different from every other person around in my family, community, and school. This made me really sad internally because I believed everyone else saw me as different and didn't accept me. I allowed the spirit of rejection to agitate me very bad until it would change my mood towards people and situations in seconds. Rejection told me that nobody loved me, and I was only tolerated by people who really didn't want me around, and sadly, I believed these things. I started to feel left out and counted out, but this was all self-inflicted because of what I "thought" people felt about me. I had to find myself in God and accept that I was loved, wanted, valued, and normal, just like everyone else around me. I had to realize that when you are accepted by God, the rejection from anyone else will never matter. I started to pray every time I felt rejected and would give it to God. Learn how to give this issue to God if you desire to get rid of it. God not only helped me defeat this huge load of sadness and rejection, but he led me to go to my mother and apologize for my actions towards her and to forgive her for anything

REAL LIFE TESTIMONIES

I believed she did to reject me in my life. It was the best feeling ever, so I encourage you to embrace deliverance, self-acceptance, and forgiveness to heal and live a happy life.

REAL LIFE TESTIMONIES

Study Scripture: 1 Peter 5:8

_____

_____

_____

_____

_____

_____

_____

_____

_____

_____

_____

_____

_____

_____

_____

_____

_____

REAL LIFE TESTIMONIES

Day 14: Stuck In The Past

When I should have been happy and living the best life, I used to allow things from the past to taunt, torment, and hinder my progression as a person overall. Every area was affected because I refused to move forward past the shame, guilt, pain, unforgiveness, and bitterness that still lived with me. I was also harboring words people used to hurt or talk about me in my heart that happened years and months ago. I wouldn't let go of the actions of others towards me, no matter how long ago they did it. I lived in the past, and for some reason, I felt entitled to do this. All I kept in my head was what I used to do, say, or where I used to go in the past, and this really hindered me from being who I am in God. I finally learned how to press past my own thoughts, the naysayers, and every memory that reminded me of my past. God began to heal and deliver me as I allowed him to free me from my past and prepare me for my future. I decided to give my past to God in exchange for my future, and I encourage you to do the same. I accepted my past, made peace with it, and lived happily and peacefully in my present. Break free from your past and live in your now. Seek God for forgiveness and be okay with whatever has happened to you or through you in your past. Your past is a part of your journey, but you do not have to live there. God loves you and desires to free you from all bondage that is holding you back from living in freedom.

REAL LIFE TESTIMONIES

Study Scripture: Revelation 12:11

REAL LIFE TESTIMONIES

Day 15: Suicide

I battled suicidal thoughts since I was a teenager, and it continued into my adult life as well. This was mainly because of the abuse I suffered mentally, emotionally, verbally, and physically from people I loved. The weight of my trauma caused me to feel as if death would be much better than living. I considered taking my own life to make this easier for everyone around me and to relieve myself from the emptiness I felt inside. I was unaware of how bright and beautiful my future would be, so the enemy tried really hard to get me to abort everything God had for me before I received it. I remember going through a deep dark depression in my life, feeling alone and as if nothing was worth living for, not even my children. There were only a few people I trusted to open up to about this because seemingly, everybody talked too much, even church folk. This spirit was getting the best of me, and it was winning. It whispered in my ear and reminded me how much wrong I had done, how much people didn't want me around, how I was hard to love, and how unimportant I was to my family and friends. These things troubled me badly. It is hard to ignore negativity about yourself when your trauma has been louder than God's voice. I remember being overwhelmed by the spirit of suicide that I fell asleep slobbering and crying. I saw myself taking a knife and stabbing myself in the stomach multiple times until it fell out of my hand. I saw my children crying in the vision and screaming because they

REAL LIFE TESTIMONIES

saw me stabbed and bleeding out. I immediately jumped up and said no way! My children need me, and they depend on me! I knew this was the moment to take my mind back and live! I started decreeing & declaring over my life like never before! I repeatedly shouted, "I shall live and not die. I shall live and declare the works of the Lord! I told the devil that he had no power to defeat me through the spirit of suicide. Your life has great meaning! Do not allow the spirit of suicide to cheat you out of abundant life in the Lord.

REAL LIFE TESTIMONIES

Study Scripture: 1 Corinthians 3:16-17

REAL LIFE TESTIMONIES

"Oh, give thanks to the Lord, for He is good! For His mercy endures forever."
~1 Chronicles 16:34

REAL LIFE TESTIMONIES

Day 16: Theft

I started stealing around in my early 20's. My boyfriend was in college, and I was a single mother without employment. My daughter always needed things, so I went out to steal them, whether it was food, clothes, shoes, or even toys to play with. I also stole to get clothes to go out and party in the clubs, and if I saw any money lying around, I took it without asking. Theft became a huge part of my character and DNA because I saw it as a quick way to survive and provide for all of my needs. I snatched and stole money and items without any thought or care. I did this for a while until my boyfriend came home, and I decided to slow down with stealing. We had a second child, and things were good financially for us, but those sticky hands were still ready if needed. One day, someone asked me to steal something for them, and I was cool with doing it, but I had no need because I had money, and I wasn't really in the mood. This person and I went to the store to shop legally, and I was picking up things to wear to church and other bay items I needed. My friend decided to do her thing and start stealing, and she kept asking me whether I was stealing as well. She left out of the store with the items she stole, but I was still shopping. Out of nowhere, the enemy spoke to me to steal the dress and purchase the rest, and I did. This was the dumbest move of my life, but it was the one that really brought clarity to me about this stealing lifestyle. My "friend" was gone, but I was being

REAL LIFE TESTIMONIES

carried to the back to be confronted and out the front in handcuffs. I was completely humiliated. This was my first offense for shoplifting, and I was able to bail myself out, but I was still embarrassed and angry about this. On my court date, I was sentenced to do ten days in jail a day before my birthday. As I approached home, my "friend" brought me the same dress I tried to steal. This really reminded me of what had happened to me, and it was time to give this lifestyle up. I prayed, confessed my sins to God, and submitted my hands to him to be purified and cleansed. I was very scared and angry about jail time, but God came through for me. I didn't serve one day, and my record was cleared from this. Repent, be delivered, and be set free! God is Real! He did It for me, and he will do it for you!

REAL LIFE TESTIMONIES

Study Scripture: Ephesians 6:11

REAL LIFE TESTIMONIES

Day 17: Trauma

In 2010 I moved to a place where I thought I could live comfortably and wouldn't have to struggle as much as I was with paying bills; instead, I was left traumatized. Just when I thought I had been through enough, bam, another incident happened in my life that caused me great pain and trauma. One day, my husband met a guy at a restaurant while purchasing food for our family. The guy spoke with my husband for a while about the church and invited him to a revival that was happening the next week. They exchanged numbers, but before ending their initial conversation, the man told my husband that God had something better for him and God wouldn't want him and his family living the way we were. Although my husband didn't reveal it to me right away, eventually, it came out. My husband was a very hardworking man, and we stayed in the streets, but this man always called to chat with him and to remind him to bring his family out for the revival. We really didn't have time for anything, but God sent us a warning. When that first night of the revival started, which was a Wednesday, I went to bingo, my cousin went her own way, and my husband went his, but we all made it back that night. The guy stopped calling about attending church, and Thursday rolled in very quickly. I went to get my hair done, my cousin went out to grab her baby some shoes, and my husband went about his normal day. However, normal mended very quickly

REAL LIFE TESTIMONIES

after we were all shot that Thursday night on our back porch. It happened so fast! We didn't see who the shooter was because his face was covered. He kept screaming out your hands up. For a split second, I thought I could get away to get help, so I tried to force my way back into the house. This caused me to get shot, my cousin got shot and collapsed, and eventually, I found out my husband had been shot as well. I didn't realize I had a bullet in my side because I was trying to get help! My husband was shot in the hip and ended up on crutches, but my cousin was shot in the torso and died on the operating table. One week after my birthday, my life was in an uproar! I was being blamed for it all, even my cousin's death. We were all close and would have never done anything to hurt each other, so the rumors and accusations were very heartbroken. It was nobody but God that saved us from dying too, and it was nobody but him to heal and comfort me through this nightmare. I was traumatized, literally. My family went through pure hell behind this, but I found peace knowing my cousin knew the truth even in her death. I could never prove anything to anyone, so I stopped trying. Don't allow trauma to dictate your happiness. Find God, lay your trauma at the altar, and grow in him as you heal in him.

REAL LIFE TESTIMONIES

Study Scripture: Ephesians 6:13

REAL LIFE TESTIMONIES

Day 18: Unforgiveness

It was tough for me to forgive people, especially those who have hurt, mistreated, and come against me. Their words and actions caused me to develop not only unforgiveness, but I was battling hatred against someone these people. This all started in my childhood because of things I experienced in my family, relationships, and friendships. I was horrible at letting things go for real. I would pretend I was over some things but then quickly snap back into rage or bitterness when I was reminded of it. This revealed that unforgiveness was still in my heart. You cannot live like this for long! Unforgiveness is cancer that will kill you slowly if you do not allow God to deliver and heal you entirely. To be free from this, I needed to be forgiven, and I also needed to be forgiven because they both works together. I encourage you to seek God through prayer to find your freedom and deliverance from this. I am free today! I can talk, love, and even fellowship with people who hurt me. Forgiveness is not about the other person; it is all about you! It is the key to your healing and breakthrough.

REAL LIFE TESTIMONIES

Study Scripture: Mark 11:25

REAL LIFE TESTIMONIES

Day 19: Overthinking

Overthinking is very unhealthy! Thinking about anything repeatedly without restraint or self-control is detrimental to your health. Please do not believe that it is okay to be an overthinker because it is not. It is clear that you are anxious, just as I was about things that were either over and gone or out of my control. I had a terrible time getting things out of my head, and it affected me mentally. If I got into a disagreement, argument, or uncomfortable conversation, I would hold the entire situation in my head and allow it to repeat over and over. I constantly talked about things that needed to be done. I held on to thoughts that were my own negativity or assumptions. Overthinking made me very moody, quick-tempered, and easily agitated. What are you overthinking? What are you allowing to set you off for no reason? This is very dangerous, and I encourage you to turn to God about this. Confess to the Lord about what you struggle with before you do something to harm others or yourself. I really fell in love with the gospel song "Deliver Me" because it ministered to me. It really helped me completely embrace my exodus from the overthinking battle that wanted my life. Avoid being anxious and antsy over things that God wants you to get rid of.

REAL LIFE TESTIMONIES

Study Scripture: Philippians 4:6

REAL LIFE TESTIMONIES

Day 20: Negativity

For decades I was negative! I had not one positive bone in my body, and it was very hard to even testify about how I made everything negative in my life. My life experiences caused me to have a corrupted mindset and character. I'm positive many people didn't like me because of my negative attitude and posture. Everything I said out of my mouth was negative, and I didn't realize how much power was in the things I released. The words I released affected me dangerously, especially all of the things I said, such as "my head hurts, I'm sick and tired, etc. These things started to manifest in my life because I spoke them into my life. They manifested just like every other negative thing I declared over my life. I spoke them so much that they became a great part of my life. I thank God I finally realized that death and life were in the power of the tongue. This was a principle in life that I needed to apply to my life. I started decreeing and declaring that I was blessed, my mindset was positive, my life was fruitful, and sickness didn't live with me anymore. I allowed God to change my perspective and help me speak and think positively no matter what distress, pain, or trauma happened in my life. Whatever we speak, we will see! Learn how to focus on the good, speak the good, and live in the good. Listen to positive affirmations, songs, and seek counseling as needed to train yourself how to see, think, and live positively.

REAL LIFE TESTIMONIES

Study Scripture: Philippians 4:8

REAL LIFE TESTIMONIES

Day 21: Health

In 2016, A few years after my son was born, I went out to eat dinner for a friend's birthday and noticed my body wasn't feeling the same. As we started to eat, things became worse for me physically, so I decided I wanted to go to the emergency room as soon as we left out. I thank God I made this decision because my glucose number was 500, and I could've literally been slipping into a diabetic coma. I was diagnosed with diabetes type 2 and prescribed meds to help me control this new diagnosis. I was very shocked but more fearful when the specialist came in and shared all these things that could happen to me with diabetes. These things were horrible and scary; I felt myself become overwhelmed. When I got home every day, I lived in fear and anxiety about my health. I was checking my numbers every other hour. I was extremely terrified about dying, losing a limb, or my vision. However, my health was declining very fast, and I couldn't do anything about it. One day, only a few days later, my vision became blurry, so I immediately made an appointment to see a doctor. I wasn't prepared, but the eye doctor told me I was losing my vision. I went into panic, started crying, and thought my life was over. I was prescribed a new pair of glasses and sent home to take it easy. It seemed as if I couldn't catch a break! My health is my wealth, and after all I had been through physically, I didn't think I could take anything else. I didn't realize that this was my cross to carry, and I needed to trust God for my healing.

REAL LIFE TESTIMONIES

Whenever he allows something to happen in our lives, we panic before we pray. Sometimes, we don't even ask him what he is trying to reveal to us through our affliction and distress. It is not easy, but it becomes easier each day that you allow God to walk with you. I was literally losing my vision, battling to lose weight, and unsure about what was next for me, but I decided to go to church despite it all. One night, during a revival, I struggled to get to the church service mentally and physically, but I made it while praise & worship was still going on. All of a sudden, the prophet called out my illness! As soon as I heard it, I ran and praised God. I shouted all over the church that night and received my healing. Although I still wear glasses, my vision is not blurred anymore, and thank God I am not blind. Be healed and trust God to be a miracle worker with your health issues.

REAL LIFE TESTIMONIES

Study Scripture: 3 John 1:2

REAL LIFE TESTIMONIES

REAL LIFE TESTIMONIES

REAL LIFE TESTIMONIES

> "The Lord is upright; He is my rock, and there is no unrighteousness in Him."
> ~Psalm 92:15

Real Life Testimonies

21-Day Inspirational Devotional

www.ingramcontent.com/pod-product-compliance
Lightning Source LLC
Chambersburg PA
CBHW060852050426
42453CB00008B/943